★ THE ★
UNITED
STATES
PRESIDENTS

JAMES
MONROE

Megan M. Gunderson

**Checkerboard
Library**

An Imprint of Abdo Publishing
abdobooks.com

ABDOBOOKS.COM

Printed in the United States of America, North Mankato, Minnesota
052020
092020

 THIS BOOK CONTAINS RECYCLED MATERIALS

Design: Emily O'Malley, Kelly Doudna, Mighty Media, Inc.
Production: Mighty Media, Inc.
Editor: Jessica Rusick

Cover Photograph: Getty Images
Interior Photographs: Albert de Bruijn/iStockphoto, p. 37; AP Images, pp. 5, 16, 36; Getty Images, p. 15; Hulton Archive/Getty Images, p. 25; ImageState/Alamy, p. 12; iStockphoto, pp. 7 (Monroe gravesite), 33; Library of Congress, pp. 6 (Elizabeth Monroe), 18, 32, 40; National Archives and Records Administration, pp. 7 (Monroe Doctrine), 29; National Archives/Getty Images, p. 31; North Wind Picture Archives/Alamy, pp. 13, 21; Pete Souza/Flickr, p. 44; Photo Researchers/Science Source, p. 17; Shutterstock Images, pp. 6, 11, 38, 39; USCapitol/Flickr, pp. 7, 23; Wikimedia Commons, pp. 26, 27, 40 (Washington), 42; Witold Skrypczak/Alamy, p. 19

Library of Congress Control Number: 2019956570

Publisher's Cataloging-in-Publication Data
Names: Gunderson, Megan M., author.
Title: James Monroe / by Megan M. Gunderson
Description: Minneapolis, Minnesota : Abdo Publishing, 2021 | Series: The United States presidents | Includes online resources and index.
Identifiers: ISBN 9781532193651 (lib. bdg.) | ISBN 9781098212292 (ebook)
Subjects: LCSH: Monroe, James, 1758-1831--Juvenile literature. | Presidents--Biography--Juvenile literature. | Presidents--United States--History--Juvenile literature. | Legislators--United States--Biography--Juvenile literature. | Politics and government--Biography--Juvenile literature.
Classification: DDC 973.54092--dc23

★ CONTENTS ★

James Monroe

James Monroe was the fifth president of the United States. He had a long political career before taking office. Today, his presidency is most remembered for the Monroe Doctrine.

Monroe grew up in Virginia. In 1774, he entered college. Two years later, he left school to fight in the **American Revolution**. Monroe fought bravely under General George Washington. After the war, he studied law.

In 1782, Monroe entered politics. He served in the Virginia House of Delegates, the Continental Congress, and the US Senate. Monroe then traveled to Europe. He was minister to France and minister to Great Britain. In 1803, he signed the Louisiana Purchase.

Monroe went on to serve as governor of Virginia. Then, he became **secretary of state** under President James Madison. During the **War of 1812**, he also served as **secretary of war**.

In 1816, Monroe was elected president. He served two terms before retiring to Virginia. Monroe had a successful presidency. His time in office became known as the Era of Good Feelings.

James Monroe

★ TIMELINE ★

1776

Monroe left school to begin fighting in the American Revolution. On December 25, Monroe crossed the Delaware River with General George Washington.

1758

On April 28, James Monroe was born in Westmoreland County, Virginia.

1786

On February 16, Monroe married Elizabeth Kortright.

1799

Monroe was elected governor of Virginia.

1774

Monroe entered the College of William and Mary in Williamsburg, Virginia.

1783

Monroe began serving in the Continental Congress.

1794

Washington nominated Monroe minister to France.

1782

Monroe was elected to the Virginia House of Delegates.

1790

Monroe was elected to the US Senate.

1811

Monroe became secretary of state under President James Madison.

1814

On September 27, Monroe replaced John Armstrong as secretary of war during the War of 1812.

1820

On March 6, Monroe signed the Missouri Compromise. Monroe was reelected president.

1831

On July 4, James Monroe died.

1803

In France, Monroe signed the Louisiana Purchase. He later became minister to Great Britain.

1816

Monroe was elected the fifth president of the United States.

1823

On December 2, Monroe gave a speech that outlined the Monroe Doctrine.

1830

Elizabeth Monroe died on September 23.

"Peace is the best time

for improvement and

preparation of every kind."

JAMES MONROE

DID YOU KNOW?

★ During James Monroe's presidency, five new states joined the nation. Mississippi became a state in 1817. Illinois joined the United States in 1818, followed by Alabama in 1819. Maine became a state the next year, followed by Missouri in 1821.

★ In 1817, Monroe became the first president to travel by steamboat.

★ One of Monroe's classmates at Campbelltown Academy in Virginia was John Marshall. Marshall became chief justice of the US Supreme Court in 1801. He served on the Court until 1835.

★ Monroe is not the only president to have died on the Fourth of July. Thomas Jefferson and John Adams both died on Independence Day in 1826.

Virginia Childhood

James Monroe was born in Westmoreland County, Virginia, on April 28, 1758. At that time, Virginia was a British colony. James had one sister and three brothers. He was the oldest son of Elizabeth Jones Monroe and Spence Monroe. Spence was a farmer and a carpenter.

At age 11, James began attending school. He went to Campbelltown Academy. There, James studied mathematics and Latin.

James liked to hunt small game birds. So, he often carried a rifle on his way to and from school. Many nights, James provided part of the family dinner!

In 1774, Spence Monroe died. As the oldest son, James was left in charge of the family property. Still, he was able to continue his education. He entered the College of William and Mary in Williamsburg, Virginia.

★ ★
★

FAST FACTS

BORN: April 28, 1758

WIFE: Elizabeth Kortright (1768–1830)

CHILDREN: 3

POLITICAL PARTY:
Democratic-Republican

AGE AT INAUGURATION: 58

YEARS SERVED: 1817–1825

VICE PRESIDENT: Daniel D. Tompkins

DIED: July 4, 1831, age 73

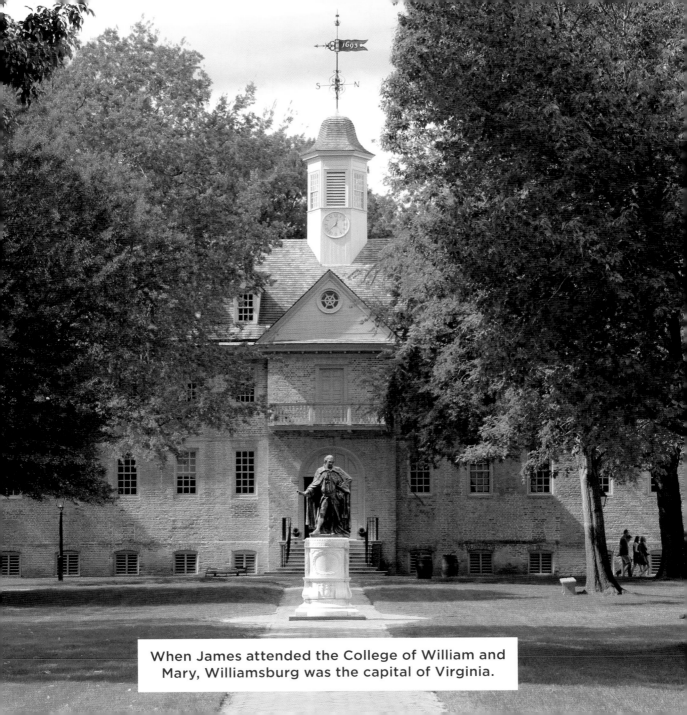

When James attended the College of William and Mary, Williamsburg was the capital of Virginia.

Joining the Fight

At the College of William and Mary, Monroe did not focus on his schoolwork. Instead, he listened to people speaking out against British rule. Monroe agreed that the colonies should break free from Britain.

So, Monroe began participating in anti-British activities. He even joined his fellow students in **raiding** the British Governor's Palace. They stole 200 guns and 300 swords.

The Governor's Palace in Williamsburg

Then, they presented the weapons to the Virginia **militia**!

In 1775, the **American Revolution** officially began. Monroe wanted to join the fight. In 1776, he left college to join the Continental army. He entered as a lieutenant in the Third Virginia **Regiment**.

The American Revolution began with the Battles of Lexington and Concord on April 19, 1775.

Meanwhile, colonial leaders approved the **Declaration of Independence** on July 4, 1776. This paper declared the colonies "Free and Independent States." But, official separation from Great Britain would only be won through years of war. So, the fight for freedom continued.

In autumn 1776, Monroe fought in two battles in New York. Then on December 25, he crossed the icy Delaware River with General George Washington. This famous crossing led to the Battle of Trenton in New Jersey.

Washington's forces captured Trenton from the **Hessians**. But during the battle, Monroe was wounded. He was shot in the shoulder and nearly died. For his bravery, Monroe was promoted to captain.

After recovering, Monroe continued to serve under General Washington. He fought in two Pennsylvania battles in 1777. On September 11, Monroe fought in the Battle of the Brandywine. Then on October 4, he fought in the Battle of Germantown. The British won both battles. Still, Monroe was promoted to major.

Next, Monroe became **aide-de-camp** to General William Alexander. In this role, he suffered through the long winter at Valley Forge. The Continental army faced cold, disease, and starvation at this Pennsylvania camp. Yet the troops did not give up.

In summer 1778, Monroe again helped General Washington in New Jersey. He served as Washington's scout before the Battle of Monmouth. Soon afterward, Monroe left the military. He then returned to Williamsburg.

In Emanuel Leutze's 1851 painting, Monroe holds the American flag as Washington leads his men across the Delaware River.

4

Politics and Family

In 1780, Monroe began studying law under Virginia governor Thomas Jefferson. The two became good friends. Along with James Madison, they worked together for many years.

Thomas Jefferson

Monroe was elected to the Virginia House of Delegates in 1782. In 1783, he began serving in the Continental Congress. This group served as the temporary US government until 1789.

In Congress, Monroe fought for navigation rights on the Mississippi River. The river was under Spanish control. But Monroe felt Americans should be able to use it for shipping goods.

Monroe also helped Jefferson write laws about developing America's western lands. Twice, Monroe traveled west to see these areas.

While serving in Congress, Monroe met Elizabeth Kortright of New York. They married on February 16, 1786.

The Monroes later had two daughters. Eliza Kortright was born in 1786. Maria Hester followed in 1803. Their son, John Spence, died very young.

The Monroe family was close. Monroe believed education was important for girls as well as boys. So, Eliza and Maria were well educated for their time.

The American Revolution ended in 1783. That same year, Monroe entered the Continental Congress.

In 1786, Monroe retired from Congress. He and his wife then moved to Fredericksburg, Virginia. That year, Monroe became a lawyer and began practicing law.

Monroe was reelected to the Virginia House of Delegates in 1787. The next year, Virginia held a **convention** to approve the new US **Constitution**.

Monroe was concerned that the Constitution did not yet include a bill of rights. He also felt it gave the national government too much power over the states. So, Monroe voted against the Constitution. Still, the convention approved it.

After the US Constitution was officially adopted,

Elizabeth Monroe

Today, the James Monroe Museum and
Memorial Library is in Fredericksburg, Virginia.
Monroe's law office once stood on this site.

Monroe supported it. It established the US Senate and the
US House of Representatives. Under this new government,
Washington was elected the first president in 1789.

5

The Diplomat

Monroe was elected to the US Senate in 1790. At the time, the **Federalist** Party controlled Congress. Monroe disagreed with the party's policies. So, he helped Jefferson and Madison form the **Democratic-Republican** Party in 1792.

Meanwhile, Great Britain and France were fighting a war. The Federalists supported Great Britain. The Democratic-Republicans feared this would damage America's relationship with France. President Washington hoped having a Democratic-Republican minister to France would avoid this. So, he nominated Monroe in 1794.

At the time, the French were upset about the Jay Treaty. This was a trade agreement between the United States and Great Britain. France worried America was favoring Britain.

In France, Monroe did not defend the treaty. So, Washington felt Monroe was not representing his country properly. He asked Monroe to return from France.

Monroe arrived home in spring 1797. He then wrote a **pamphlet** attacking President Washington. It was published in December.

Monroe's anti-Washington pamphlet is titled *A View of the Conduct of the Executive, in Foreign Affairs of the United States*.

In 1799, Monroe was elected governor of Virginia. He served in this position until 1802. As governor, Monroe supported public education. He also promoted Jefferson for president in the election of 1800.

Jefferson became the third US president in 1801. In January 1803, he decided to send Monroe back to France. The United States wanted to purchase New Orleans from France. This area of Louisiana was important to US trade.

Monroe arrived in France on April 12. There, he assisted US minister to France Robert Livingston. Monroe was surprised to learn France was willing to sell all of Louisiana. On May 2, Monroe and Livingston signed the Louisiana Purchase. This doubled the size of the United States.

Meanwhile, Monroe had been named minister to Great Britain. In July, he went to London. At the time, Britain was seizing US ships and forcing US sailors into service. So, Jefferson had Monroe discuss possible solutions with the British.

The result was a treaty. Monroe signed it on December 31, 1806. However, Jefferson felt the treaty did not do enough to protect American ships. So, he rejected it. Monroe then returned home in December 1807.

LOUISIANA PURCHASE, 1803

The third signing of the Louisiana Treaty, which officially
transferred the new land to the United States

Secretary of State

In November 1811, Monroe became **secretary of state under President Madison**. At the time, the British were still attacking US ships. Madison and Monroe felt war was necessary. On June 18, 1812, Congress declared war on Great Britain. This was the beginning of the **War of 1812**.

In August 1814, the British captured Washington, DC. President Madison blamed **Secretary of War** John Armstrong for not preventing the attack. On September 27, he replaced Armstrong with Monroe. Now, Monroe held two **cabinet** positions at once!

On December 24, the United States and Great Britain signed the Treaty of Ghent. With this, the countries agreed to end the war. In 1815, Monroe stepped down as secretary of war. He remained secretary of state for two more years.

Many people respected Monroe's leadership during the war. In 1816, he ran for president. Monroe easily defeated **Federalist** Rufus King. He won 183 electoral votes to King's 34. Governor of New York Daniel D. Tompkins was elected vice president.

Vice President Daniel D. Tompkins

7

President Monroe

Monroe was **inaugurated** as the fifth US president on March 4, 1817. The White House had been burned during the **War of 1812**. So, the Monroe family could not move in until September 1817. In the meantime, Monroe traveled around the nation. This helped Americans get to know their president.

Osceola was one of the Seminole leaders during the First Seminole War.

★ ★
★
SUPREME COURT APPOINTMENT

SMITH THOMPSON: 1823

When Monroe took office, there was trouble on the border between Georgia and Florida. At the time, Spain controlled Florida. Runaway slaves and Seminole Native Americans from Florida were attacking US towns.

So, Monroe sent General Andrew Jackson to stop the attacks. Jackson invaded Florida. There, he fought what became known as the First Seminole War.

Secretary of State John Quincy Adams then organized a treaty with Spain. The Transcontinental Treaty was signed in 1819. In it, Spain agreed to give Florida to the United States. Spain also gave up any claims to the Oregon Territory. In exchange, the United States recognized Spanish authority over the territory of Texas.

John Quincy Adams

Meanwhile, Americans had begun arguing about slavery. On March 6, 1820, President Monroe signed the Missouri Compromise.

The compromise admitted Maine as a free state and Missouri as a slave state. And, it banned slavery in the northern part of the Louisiana Territory. This kept a balance between slave and free states represented in the Senate. Temporarily, Americans on both sides of the slavery issue were satisfied.

Later that year, Monroe was reelected president. The next year, March 4 was a Sunday. So, Monroe was **inaugurated** on March 5, 1821.

During his second term, President Monroe gave one of his most famous speeches. In Congress on December 2, 1823, Monroe outlined what would become the Monroe Doctrine.

At the time, the United States feared that Spain would try to reclaim some of its former colonies. And, the United States worried Russia wanted to take over land in northwestern North America.

Monroe responded to these threats in his speech. He said North and South America were free. Europe should not try to establish new colonies there. Also, he said the nation would see attacks on its neighbors as threats to the United States. In return, he promised not to interfere in European wars.

The Monroe Doctrine is one of the most important elements of Monroe's presidency. Long after he left office, US presidents continued to follow its ideas.

The Monroe Doctrine came from the president's
seventh annual address to Congress.

PRESIDENT MONROE'S CABINET

FIRST TERM

March 4, 1817–March 5, 1821

- ★ **STATE:** John Quincy Adams
- ★ **TREASURY:** William H. Crawford
- ★ **WAR:** John C. Calhoun
- ★ **NAVY:** Benjamin W. Crowninshield
  Smith Thompson (from January 1, 1819)
- ★ **ATTORNEY GENERAL:** Richard Rush
  William Wirt (from November 15, 1817)

SECOND TERM

March 5, 1821–March 4, 1825

- ★ **STATE:** John Quincy Adams
- ★ **TREASURY:** William H. Crawford
- ★ **WAR:** John C. Calhoun
- ★ **NAVY:** Smith Thompson
  Samuel L. Southard (from September 16, 1823)
- ★ **ATTORNEY GENERAL:** William Wirt

President James Monroe

8

Retirement

President Monroe decided not to run for a third term. In 1824, three of his **cabinet** members ran for president! Secretary Adams won the election. **Secretary of War** John C. Calhoun was elected vice president.

In 1825, the Monroes retired to Leesburg, Virginia. Their new home was called Oak Hill. The following year, Monroe became a **regent** of the University of Virginia. Jefferson had founded this school in Charlottesville in 1819.

Oak Hill is now a US National Historic Landmark.

Monroe became president of Virginia's **constitutional convention** in 1829. There, he helped amend the state constitution. This was Monroe's last public office.

On September 23, 1830, Elizabeth Monroe died at Oak Hill. Monroe missed her very much. So, that year, he sold his home and moved to New York City. He lived there with his daughter Maria while his health weakened. James Monroe died on July 4, 1831.

Monroe had a successful career in state and national politics. He helped with foreign relations as minister to France and minister to Great Britain. He continued this work as **secretary of state**.

Monroe's grave site in Richmond, Virginia

As president, Monroe signed the Missouri Compromise. And, he introduced the Monroe Doctrine. James Monroe's contributions had a lasting effect on the United States.

BRANCHES OF GOVERNMENT

The US government is divided into three branches. They are the executive, legislative, and judicial branches. This division is called a separation of powers. Each branch has some power over the others. This is called a system of checks and balances.

★ EXECUTIVE BRANCH

The executive branch enforces laws. It is made up of the president, the vice president, and the president's cabinet. The president represents the United States around the world. He or she oversees relations with other countries and signs treaties. The president signs bills into law and appoints officials and federal judges. He or she also leads the military and manages government workers.

★ LEGISLATIVE BRANCH

The legislative branch makes laws, maintains the military, and regulates trade. It also has the power to declare war. This branch consists of the Senate and the House of Representatives. Together, these two houses make up Congress. Each state has two senators. A state's population determines the number of representatives it has.

★ JUDICIAL BRANCH

The judicial branch interprets laws. It consists of district courts, courts of appeals, and the Supreme Court. District courts try cases. If a person disagrees with a trial's outcome, he or she may appeal. If a court of appeals supports the ruling, a person may appeal to the Supreme Court. The Supreme Court also makes sure that laws follow the US Constitution.

THE PRESIDENT ★

★ QUALIFICATIONS FOR OFFICE

To be president, a person must meet three requirements. A candidate must be at least 35 years old and a natural-born US citizen. He or she must also have lived in the United States for at least 14 years.

★ ELECTORAL COLLEGE

The US presidential election is an indirect election. Voters from each state choose electors to represent them in the Electoral College. The number of electors from each state is based on the state's population. Each elector has one electoral vote. Electors are pledged to cast their vote for the candidate who receives the highest number of popular votes in their state. A candidate must receive the majority of Electoral College votes to win.

★ TERM OF OFFICE

Each president may be elected to two four-year terms. Sometimes, a president may only be elected once. This happens if he or she served more than two years of the previous president's term.

The presidential election is held on the Tuesday after the first Monday in November. The president is sworn in on January 20 of the following year. At that time, he or she takes the oath of office:

> *I do solemnly swear (or affirm) that I will faithfully execute the office of President of the United States, and will to the best of my ability, preserve, protect and defend the Constitution of the United States.*

★ LINE OF SUCCESSION ★

The Presidential Succession Act of 1947 defines who becomes president if the president cannot serve. The vice president is first in the line of succession. Next are the Speaker of the House and the President Pro Tempore of the Senate. If none of these individuals is able to serve, the office falls to the president's cabinet members. They would take office in the order in which each department was created:

Secretary of State

Secretary of the Treasury

Secretary of Defense

Attorney General

Secretary of the Interior

Secretary of Agriculture

Secretary of Commerce

Secretary of Labor

Secretary of Health and Human Services

Secretary of Housing and Urban Development

Secretary of Transportation

Secretary of Energy

Secretary of Education

Secretary of Veterans Affairs

Secretary of Homeland Security

While in office, the president receives a salary of $400,000 each year. He or she lives in the White House and has 24-hour Secret Service protection.

The president may travel on a Boeing 747 jet called Air Force One. The airplane can accommodate 76 passengers. It has kitchens, a dining room, sleeping areas, and a conference room. It also has fully equipped offices with the latest communications systems. Air Force One can fly halfway around the world before needing to refuel. It can even refuel in flight!

Air Force One

If the president wishes to travel by car, he or she uses Cadillac One. It has been modified with heavy armor and communications systems. The president takes

Cadillac One

Cadillac One along when visiting other countries if secure transportation will be needed.

The president also travels on a helicopter called Marine One. Like the presidential car, Marine One accompanies the president when traveling abroad if necessary.

Sometimes, the president needs to get away and relax with family and friends. Camp David is the official presidential retreat. It is located in the cool, wooded mountains of Maryland. The US Navy maintains the retreat, and the US Marine Corps keeps it secure. The camp offers swimming, tennis, golf, and hiking.

When the president leaves office, he or she receives lifetime Secret Service protection. He or she also receives a yearly pension of $207,800 and funding for office space, supplies, and staff.

Marine One

George Washington

Abraham Lincoln

Theodore Roosevelt

	PRESIDENT	PARTY	TOOK OFFICE
1	George Washington	None	April 30, 1789
2	John Adams	Federalist	March 4, 1797
3	Thomas Jefferson	Democratic-Republican	March 4, 1801
4	James Madison	Democratic-Republican	March 4, 1809
5	James Monroe	Democratic-Republican	March 4, 1817
6	John Quincy Adams	Democratic-Republican	March 4, 1825
7	Andrew Jackson	Democrat	March 4, 1829
8	Martin Van Buren	Democrat	March 4, 1837
9	William H. Harrison	Whig	March 4, 1841
10	John Tyler	Whig	April 6, 1841
11	James K. Polk	Democrat	March 4, 1845
12	Zachary Taylor	Whig	March 5, 1849
13	Millard Fillmore	Whig	July 10, 1850
14	Franklin Pierce	Democrat	March 4, 1853
15	James Buchanan	Democrat	March 4, 1857
16	Abraham Lincoln	Republican	March 4, 1861
17	Andrew Johnson	Democrat	April 15, 1865
18	Ulysses S. Grant	Republican	March 4, 1869
19	Rutherford B. Hayes	Republican	March 3, 1877

THEIR TERMS ★

LEFT OFFICE	TERMS SERVED	VICE PRESIDENT
March 4, 1797	Two	John Adams
March 4, 1801	One	Thomas Jefferson
March 4, 1809	Two	Aaron Burr, George Clinton
March 4, 1817	Two	George Clinton, Elbridge Gerry
March 4, 1825	Two	Daniel D. Tompkins
March 4, 1829	One	John C. Calhoun
March 4, 1837	Two	John C. Calhoun, Martin Van Buren
March 4, 1841	One	Richard M. Johnson
April 4, 1841	Died During First Term	John Tyler
March 4, 1845	Completed Harrison's Term	Office Vacant
March 4, 1849	One	George M. Dallas
July 9, 1850	Died During First Term	Millard Fillmore
March 4, 1853	Completed Taylor's Term	Office Vacant
March 4, 1857	One	William R.D. King
March 4, 1861	One	John C. Breckinridge
April 15, 1865	Served One Term, Died During Second Term	Hannibal Hamlin, Andrew Johnson
March 4, 1869	Completed Lincoln's Second Term	Office Vacant
March 4, 1877	Two	Schuyler Colfax, Henry Wilson
March 4, 1881	One	William A. Wheeler

Franklin D. Roosevelt

John F. Kennedy

Ronald Reagan

	PRESIDENT	PARTY	TOOK OFFICE
20	James A. Garfield	Republican	March 4, 1881
21	Chester Arthur	Republican	September 20, 1881
22	Grover Cleveland	Democrat	March 4, 1885
23	Benjamin Harrison	Republican	March 4, 1889
24	Grover Cleveland	Democrat	March 4, 1893
25	William McKinley	Republican	March 4, 1897
26	Theodore Roosevelt	Republican	September 14, 1901
27	William Taft	Republican	March 4, 1909
28	Woodrow Wilson	Democrat	March 4, 1913
29	Warren G. Harding	Republican	March 4, 1921
30	Calvin Coolidge	Republican	August 3, 1923
31	Herbert Hoover	Republican	March 4, 1929
32	Franklin D. Roosevelt	Democrat	March 4, 1933
33	Harry S. Truman	Democrat	April 12, 1945
34	Dwight D. Eisenhower	Republican	January 20, 1953
35	John F. Kennedy	Democrat	January 20, 1961

LEFT OFFICE	TERMS SERVED	VICE PRESIDENT
September 19, 1881	Died During First Term	Chester Arthur
March 4, 1885	Completed Garfield's Term	Office Vacant
March 4, 1889	One	Thomas A. Hendricks
March 4, 1893	One	Levi P. Morton
March 4, 1897	One	Adlai E. Stevenson
September 14, 1901	Served One Term, Died During Second Term	Garret A. Hobart, Theodore Roosevelt
March 4, 1909	Completed McKinley's Second Term, Served One Term	Office Vacant, Charles Fairbanks
March 4, 1913	One	James S. Sherman
March 4, 1921	Two	Thomas R. Marshall
August 2, 1923	Died During First Term	Calvin Coolidge
March 4, 1929	Completed Harding's Term, Served One Term	Office Vacant, Charles Dawes
March 4, 1933	One	Charles Curtis
April 12, 1945	Served Three Terms, Died During Fourth Term	John Nance Garner, Henry A. Wallace, Harry S. Truman
January 20, 1953	Completed Roosevelt's Fourth Term, Served One Term	Office Vacant, Alben Barkley
January 20, 1961	Two	Richard Nixon
November 22, 1963	Died During First Term	Lyndon B. Johnson

	PRESIDENT	PARTY	TOOK OFFICE
36	Lyndon B. Johnson	Democrat	November 22, 1963
37	Richard Nixon	Republican	January 20, 1969
38	Gerald Ford	Republican	August 9, 1974
39	Jimmy Carter	Democrat	January 20, 1977
40	Ronald Reagan	Republican	January 20, 1981
41	George H.W. Bush	Republican	January 20, 1989
42	Bill Clinton	Democrat	January 20, 1993
43	George W. Bush	Republican	January 20, 2001
44	Barack Obama	Democrat	January 20, 2009
45	Donald Trump	Republican	January 20, 2017

Barack Obama

★ PRESIDENTS MATH GAME ★

Have fun with this presidents math game! First, study the list above and memorize each president's name and number. Then, use math to figure out which president completes each equation below.

1. Lyndon B. Johnson − James Monroe = ?

2. James Monroe + Andrew Johnson = ?

3. Millard Fillmore − James Monroe = ?

Answers: 1. Herbert Hoover (36 − 5 = 31)
2. Grover Cleveland (5 + 17 = 22)
3. Martin Van Buren (13 − 5 = 8)

LEFT OFFICE	TERMS SERVED	VICE PRESIDENT
January 20, 1969	Completed Kennedy's Term, Served One Term	Office Vacant, Hubert H. Humphrey
August 9, 1974	Completed First Term, Resigned During Second Term	Spiro T. Agnew, Gerald Ford
January 20, 1977	Completed Nixon's Second Term	Nelson A. Rockefeller
January 20, 1981	One	Walter Mondale
January 20, 1989	Two	George H.W. Bush
January 20, 1993	One	Dan Quayle
January 20, 2001	Two	Al Gore
January 20, 2009	Two	Dick Cheney
January 20, 2017	Two	Joe Biden
		Mike Pence

★ WRITE TO THE PRESIDENT ★

You may write to the president at:

**The White House
1600 Pennsylvania Avenue NW
Washington, DC 20500**

You may email the president at:

www.whitehouse.gov/contact

★ GLOSSARY ★

aide-de-camp—a military officer who acts as an assistant to an officer with a higher rank.

American Revolution—from 1775 to 1783. A war for independence between Great Britain and its North American colonies. The colonists won and created the United States of America.

cabinet—a group of advisers chosen by the president to lead government departments.

constitution—the laws that govern a country or a state. The US Constitution is the laws that govern the United States. Something relating to or following the laws of a constitution is constitutional.

convention—a group of people meeting for a special purpose.

Declaration of Independence—an essay written at the Second Continental Congress in 1776, announcing the separation of the American colonies from England.

Democratic-Republican—a member of the Democratic-Republican political party. During the early 1800s, Democratic-Republicans believed in weak national government and strong state government.

Federalist—a member of the Federalist political party. During the early 1800s, Federalists believed in a strong national government.

Hessian—a German soldier serving for the British during the American Revolution.

inaugurate (ih-NAW-gyuh-rayt)—to swear into a political office.

militia (muh-LIH-shuh)—a group of citizens trained for war or emergencies.

pamphlet (PAM-fluht)—a printed publication without a cover.

raid—to conduct a surprise attack.

regent—a member of a governing board.

regiment—a large military unit made up of troops.

secretary of state—a member of the president's cabinet who handles relations with other countries.

secretary of war— a member of the president's cabinet who handles the nation's defense. This position was replaced by the secretary of the army in 1947.

War of 1812—from 1812 to 1815. A war fought between the United States and Great Britain over shipping rights and the capture of US soldiers.

ONLINE RESOURCES

To learn more about James Monroe, please visit **abdobooklinks.com** or scan this QR code. These links are routinely monitored and updated to provide the most current information available.

★ INDEX ★